GW00787432

KS2 Maths
Learning Aid

Improving understanding through colour and clarity

Get your FREE digital book!

This book includes a free digital edition for use on computers (PC and Mac), tablets or smartphones.

Go to ddedu.co.uk/maths-ks2
and enter this code...

Code: DPPJJU66

Contents

Ratio and Proportion 3:4

Algebra $2x = 6$

Measurement

Properties of Shapes

Position and Direction

Statistics

Maths Jargon

Symbols

✚	Addition	$4 + 3 = 7$
▬	Subtraction	$7 - 5 = 2$
✖	Multiplication	$2 \times 4 = 8$
➗	Division	$12 \div 3 = 4$
▬	Is equal to	$\frac{1}{2} = 0.5$
≢	Is not equal to	$3 \neq 4$
≈	Approximate	$a \approx 4{,}000$

Inequalities

$1 < 3$
1 is less than 3

$3 > 1$
3 is more than 1

≤ Less than or equal to
$y \leq 5$ y is less than or equal to 5

≥ More than or equal to
$y \geq 7$ y is more than or equal to 7

Factors

Every number has **FACTORS**.
The **FACTORS** of **12** are **1, 2, 3, 4, 6** and **12**
because all of these numbers go exactly into 12.

Prime Numbers

2, 3, 5, 7, 11, 13, 17...

PRIME NUMBERS have only 2 factors, themselves and 1.
PRIME FACTORS are factors which are also prime numbers.
For example, 2 and 3 are prime factors of 12.

Square Numbers

The product of a number multiplied by itself.

1^2
$1 \times 1 = 1$

2^2
$2 \times 2 = 4$

3^2
$3 \times 3 = 9$

Cube Numbers

The product of a number multiplied by itself 3 times.

1^3
$1 \times 1 \times 1 = 1$

2^3
$2 \times 2 \times 2 = 8$

3^3
$3 \times 3 \times 3 = 27$

Multiples

Every number has **MULTIPLES**. For example, every number that 3 goes into is a **MULTIPLE** of 3, so 3, 6, 9, 12, 15,18... etc. are all multiples of 3.

daydrea
EDUCAT

Place Value

Thousands 1000s	Hundreds 100s	Tens 10s	Ones 1s	Decimal Point	Tenths 1/10	Hundredths 1/100	Thousandths 1/1000
1	6	8	2	●	4	7	3
Whole numbers with a value of 0 or more					Numbers with a value of less than 1		

Look at what each digit in the numbers below represent.

324
is made up of:
3 hundreds
2 tens
4 ones

46
is made up of:
4 tens
6 ones

6457
is made up of:
6 thousands
4 hundreds
5 tens
7 ones

2.45
is made up of:
2 ones
4 tenths
5 hundredths

Look at the numbers below. What does the digit 4 in each number represent? Can you put the numbers in order from smallest to largest?

34   426   748   8421   304   3.04   7.46

Adding and Subtracting by Powers of 10

To **increase** a number by one thousand, add one to the thousands digit.
3482 + 1000 = 4482

To **increase** a number by one hundred, add one to the hundreds digit.
3482 + 100 = 3582

To **increase** a number by ten, add one to the tens digit.
3482 + 10 = 3492

Thousands 1000s	Hundreds 100s	Tens 10s	Ones 1s
3	4	8	2

To **decrease** a number by one thousand, subtract one from the thousands digit.
3482 - 1000 = 2482

To **decrease** a number by one hundred, subtract one from the hundreds digit.
3482 - 100 = 3382

To **decrease** a number by ten, subtract one from the tens digit.
3482 - 10 = 3472

What happens if the digit you're adding to is 9?
If you add one to nine you get ten: 9 + 1 = 10.
The same rule applies when adding other powers of 10.

To add 10 to 3492:
Add one to the hundreds digit and change the tens digit to zero.
3492 + 10 = 3502
You've gone from 49 tens to 50 tens.

To add 100 to 3982:
Add one to the thousands digit and change the hundreds digit to zero.
3982 + 100 = 4082
You've gone from 39 hundreds to 40 hundreds.

Rounding Numbers

It is not always necessary to use exact numbers, so rounding is used to provide simpler numbers that are easier to use.

Rounding Using a Number Line

Number lines are used to help determine whether to round a number up or down.

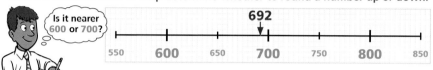

692 rounded to the nearest hundred is **700**.
The number line shows that **692** is closer to **700** than it is to **600**.

To round **2743** to the nearest ten, you need to identify whether it is nearer 40 or 50.

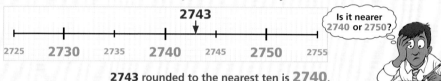

2743 rounded to the nearest ten is **2740**.
The number line shows that **2743** is closer to **2740** than it is to **2750**.

The same rule applies when rounding to decimal places.

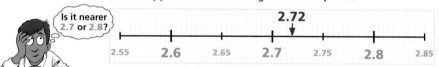

2.72 rounded to one decimal place is **2.7**.
The number line shows that **2.72** is closer to **2.7** than it is to **2.8**.
When rounding numbers to decimal places, only consider the digits **after** the decimal point.

Rounding Without a Number Line

Without a number line, look at the **first digit to the right** of the digit you are rounding.

If the number is less than 5, leave it alone.

1734 rounded to the nearest hundred is **1700**.
— *less than 5 – leave it alone*

53.41 rounded to the nearest whole number is **53**.
— *less than 5 – leave it alone*

If the number is 5 or more, round up.

77 rounded to the nearest ten is **80**.
— *5 or more – round up*

3.14159 rounded to three decimal places is **3.142**.
— *5 or more – round up*

daydrea
EDUCAT

Negative Numbers

A negative number is any number that is less than zero.
Negative numbers are denoted by a minus sign, −.

The number line below shows the integers, or whole numbers, from -10 to 10.

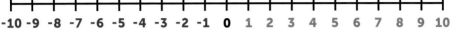

Negative Numbers   **Positive Numbers**

-10 -9 -8 -7 -6 -5 -4 -3 -2 -1 0 1 2 3 4 5 6 7 8 9 10

◄──── Smaller ──────────────────── Larger ────►

Numbers to the **left** on a number line are smaller than those to their **right**. The value of negative numbers decreases from right to left. For example, -7 is less than -2.

Real-life examples of negative numbers include:

    Temperature │ **Bank Balances**

The following rules apply when adding or subtracting negative numbers.

Adding a negative number is the same as subtracting. It produces a lower value.

$$2 \boxed{+ \text{-}3} = \text{-}1$$

+ -3

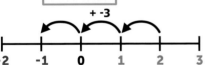

-2   -1   0   1   2   3

If you **add a negative number**, you move to the **left** on a number line.

Subtracting a negative number is the same as adding. It produces a higher value.

$$4 \boxed{- \text{-}2} = 6$$

- -2

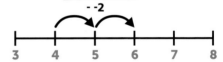

3   4   5   6   7   8

If you **subtract a negative number**, you move to the **right** on a number line.

The following rules apply when multiplying or dividing negative numbers.

$$2 \times \text{-}3 = \text{-}6$$

Multiplying a **positive number** by a **negative number** (and vice versa) produces a **negative number**.

$$21 \div \text{-}3 = \text{-}7$$

Dividing a **positive number** by a **negative number** (and vice versa) produces a **negative number**.

$$\text{-}2 \times \text{-}3 = 6$$

Multiplying **two negative numbers** produces a **positive number**.

$$\text{-}18 \div \text{-}3 = 6$$

Dividing a **negative number** by a **negative number** produces a **positive number**.

ROMAN NUMERALS

The main set of Roman numerals are:

I	V	X	L	C	D	M
1	**5**	**10**	**50**	**100**	**500**	**1000**

All other Roman numerals are made up of the above symbols.

II = 2
(two ones)

VI = 6
(one after five)

XIX = 19
(one before 20)

III = 3
(three ones)

VIII = 8
(three after five)

XC = 90
(ten before 100)

IV = 4
(one before five)

XI = 11
(one after ten)

DXV = 515
(500 + 10 + 5)

TIME

Roman numerals are sometimes used on clocks to replace the numbers 1–12.

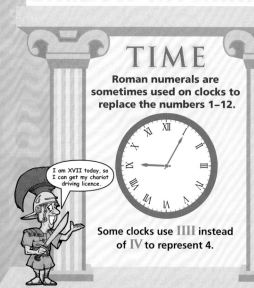

I am XVII today, so I can get my chariot driving licence.

Some clocks use **IIII** instead of **IV** to represent 4.

YEARS

Roman numerals are sometimes used to represent the year.

MDCCCXC

I am LXV today, so I can get my free public chariot pass.

This building was built in 1890.
MDCCCXC = 1890
1000 + 500 + 100 + 100 + 100 + 90

daydream EDUCATION

Column Addition

It is not always possible to perform addition in your head.
In such instances, column addition should be used.

To solve this addition problem,
follow the steps outlined below.

56 + 272 + 191

1 List all numbers underneath one another, so that digits with the same place value (hundreds, tens, ones) are aligned vertically.

```
  H  T  O
     5  6
  2  7  2
+ 1  9  1
---------
```

2 When performing column addition, always work from **right to left**.

Add the numbers in the ones column first.

6 + 2 + 1 = **9**

Write the answer underneath the numbers that are being added together.

```
  H  T  O
     5  6
  2  7  2
+ 1  9  1
---------
        9
```

3 Add the numbers in the tens column.

5 + 7 + 9 = **21**

If the answer has two digits, the second digit, 1, is written underneath the numbers that are being added together, and the first digit, 2, which represents two hundred, is carried over to the hundreds column.

Write the carried number here.

```
  H  T  O
     5  6
  2  7  2
+ 1  9  1
---------
     1  9
  2
```

4 Add the numbers in the hundreds column, and remember to include any carried numbers.

2 + 1 + 2 (the carried number) = **5**

Write the answer underneath the numbers that are being added together. The addition is now complete.

Remember to add me!

```
  H  T  O
     5  6
  2  7  2
+ 1  9  1
---------
  5  1  9
  2
```

56 + 272 + 191 = **519**

daydream EDUCATION

11

Column Subtraction

It is not always possible to perform subtraction in your head. In such instances, column subtraction should be used.

To solve this subtraction problem, follow the steps outlined below.

639 – 271

1

List the number being subtracted, 271, **under** the other number, 639, so that digits with the same place value (hundreds, tens, ones) are aligned vertically.

```
  H  T  O
  6  3  9
- 2  7  1
----------
```

2

When performing column subtraction, always work from **right to left**.

Subtract the numbers in the ones column first.

9 – 1 = 8

Write the answer underneath the ones column.

```
  H  T  O
  6  3  9
- 2  7  1
----------
        8
```

3

Subtract the numbers in the tens column. If the top number is smaller than the bottom number, take 1 from the column to the left (hundreds).

More on the floor? Go next door and get 10 more!

Because 3 is smaller than 7, take 1 from the hundreds column. The 6 in the hundreds column becomes 5, and the 3 in the tens column becomes 13.

13 – 7 = 6

```
   5   13
   6    3  9
-  2    7  1
-------------
        6  8
```

4

Subtract the numbers in the hundreds column, and write the answer underneath.

5 – 2 = 3

The subtraction is now complete.

639 – 271 = 368

```
   5   13
   6    3  9
-  2    7  1
-------------
   3    6  8
```

daydream EDUCATION

Multiplication

✕	1	2	3	4	5	6	7	8	9	10	11	12
1	1	2	3	4	5	6	7	8	9	10	11	12
2	2	4	6	8	10	12	14	16	18	20	22	24
3	3	6	9	12	15	18	21	24	27	30	33	36
4	4	8	12	16	20	24	28	32	36	40	44	48
5	5	10	15	20	25	30	35	40	45	50	55	60
6	6	12	18	24	30	36	42	48	54	60	66	72
7	7	14	21	28	35	42	49	56	63	70	77	84
8	8	16	24	32	40	48	56	64	72	80	88	96
9	9	18	27	36	45	54	63	72	81	90	99	108
10	10	20	30	40	50	60	70	80	90	100	110	120
11	11	22	33	44	55	66	77	88	99	110	121	132
12	12	24	36	48	60	72	84	96	108	120	132	144

Spot the Patterns

The numbers in the **ORANGE** squares are all square numbers.
Notice that **3 × 8 = 24** and **8 × 3 = 24**
Can you spot any other patterns? The figures in the **GREEN** squares form one pattern, but there are many more.

daydream EDUCATION

Times Tables 1-6

There are not as many to learn as you think!

One

1 × 1 =	1
2 × 1 =	2
3 × 1 =	3
4 × 1 =	4
5 × 1 =	5
6 × 1 =	6
7 × 1 =	7
8 × 1 =	8
9 × 1 =	9
10 × 1 =	10
11 × 1 =	11
12 × 1 =	12

Two

1 × 2 =	2
2 × 2 =	4
3 × 2 =	6
4 × 2 =	8
5 × 2 =	10
6 × 2 =	12
7 × 2 =	14
8 × 2 =	16
9 × 2 =	18
10 × 2 =	20
11 × 2 =	22
12 × 2 =	24

Three

1 × 3 =	3
2 × 3 =	6
3 × 3 =	9
4 × 3 =	12
5 × 3 =	15
6 × 3 =	18
7 × 3 =	21
8 × 3 =	24
9 × 3 =	27
10 × 3 =	30
11 × 3 =	33
12 × 3 =	36

Four

1 × 4 =	4
2 × 4 =	8
3 × 4 =	12
4 × 4 =	16
5 × 4 =	20
6 × 4 =	24
7 × 4 =	28
8 × 4 =	32
9 × 4 =	36
10 × 4 =	40
11 × 4 =	44
12 × 4 =	48

Five

1 × 5 =	5
2 × 5 =	10
3 × 5 =	15
4 × 5 =	20
5 × 5 =	25
6 × 5 =	30
7 × 5 =	35
8 × 5 =	40
9 × 5 =	45
10 × 5 =	50
11 × 5 =	55
12 × 5 =	60

Six

1 × 6 =	6
2 × 6 =	12
3 × 6 =	18
4 × 6 =	24
5 × 6 =	30
6 × 6 =	36
7 × 6 =	42
8 × 6 =	48
9 × 6 =	54
10 × 6 =	60
11 × 6 =	66
12 × 6 =	72

The numbers in orange are the ones you've already learnt.
If you look closely they have appeared in a previous table.

The numbers in boxes are called square numbers. Why? 4 × 4 = 16

Times Tables 7-12

There are not as many to learn as you think!

Seven

1	× 7	=	7
2	× 7	=	14
3	× 7	=	21
4	× 7	=	28
5	× 7	=	35
6	× 7	=	42
7	× 7	=	[49]
8	× 7	=	56
9	× 7	=	63
10	× 7	=	70
11	× 7	=	77
12	× 7	=	84

Eight

1	× 8	=	8
2	× 8	=	16
3	× 8	=	24
4	× 8	=	32
5	× 8	=	40
6	× 8	=	48
7	× 8	=	56
8	× 8	=	[64]
9	× 8	=	72
10	× 8	=	80
11	× 8	=	88
12	× 8	=	96

Nine

1	× 9	=	9
2	× 9	=	18
3	× 9	=	27
4	× 9	=	36
5	× 9	=	45
6	× 9	=	54
7	× 9	=	63
8	× 9	=	72
9	× 9	=	[81]
10	× 9	=	90
11	× 9	=	99
12	× 9	=	108

Ten

1	×10	=	10
2	×10	=	20
3	×10	=	30
4	×10	=	40
5	×10	=	50
6	×10	=	60
7	×10	=	70
8	×10	=	80
9	×10	=	90
10	×10	=	[100]
11	×10	=	110
12	×10	=	120

Eleven

1	×11	=	11
2	×11	=	22
3	×11	=	33
4	×11	=	44
5	×11	=	55
6	×11	=	66
7	×11	=	77
8	×11	=	88
9	×11	=	99
10	×11	=	110
11	×11	=	[121]
12	×11	=	132

Twelve

1	×12	=	12
2	×12	=	24
3	×12	=	36
4	×12	=	48
5	×12	=	60
6	×12	=	72
7	×12	=	84
8	×12	=	96
9	×12	=	108
10	×12	=	120
11	×12	=	132
12	×12	=	[144]

The numbers in orange are the ones you've already learnt.
If you look closely they have appeared in a previous table.

The numbers in boxes are called square numbers. Why?  8 × 8 = 64

Prime Numbers

A **prime number** is a whole number that has only **two** factors: itself and 1.
For example, **7** is a prime number because it has only **two** factors: 7 and 1.

$$7 \div 7 = 1$$ and $$7 \div 1 = 7$$

1	2	3	4	5	6	7	8	9	10
11	12	13	14	15	16	17	18	19	20
21	22	23	24	25	26	27	28	29	30
31	32	33	34	35	36	37	38	39	40
41	42	43	44	45	46	47	48	49	50
51	52	53	54	55	56	57	58	59	60
61	62	63	64	65	66	67	68	69	70
71	72	73	74	75	76	77	78	79	80
81	82	83	84	85	86	87	88	89	90
91	92	93	94	95	96	97	98	99	100

Prime-mates

13 is a **prime number**.
It has **two** factors: 13 and 1.
$13 \div 1 = 13$ $13 \div 13 = 1$

2 is the lowest and only even **prime number**.
It has **two** factors: 2 and 1.
$2 \div 1 = 2$ $2 \div 2 = 1$

1 is **not** a prime number.
It has only **one** factor: 1.
$1 \div 1 = 1$

   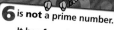

6 is **not** a prime number.
It has **four** factors:
1, 2, 3 and 6.
$6 \div 1 = 6$ $6 \div 2 = 3$
$6 \div 3 = 2$ $6 \div 6 = 1$

daydream EDUCATI

Short Division

It is not always possible to solve division problems mentally. In such instances short division can be used.

To solve this division problem, follow the steps outlined below.

The number being divided is called the dividend. → $8192 \div 4$ ← The number by which the dividend is divided is called the divisor.

The answer to a division problem is called the **quotient**.

1 Rewrite the division problem so that the dividend (8192) is written in a division bracket and the divisor (4) is written to the left of the bracket.

$4\overline{)8\ 1\ 9\ 2}$

2 Short division is performed from left to right, so divide the first digit in the dividend (8) by the divisor (4).

4 goes into 8 twice: $8 \div 4 = 2$

Write 2 directly above the first digit in the dividend.

$\begin{array}{r} 2 \\ 4\overline{)8\ 1\ 9\ 2} \end{array}$

3 Divide the next digit in the dividend by the divisor. In this instance, 4 does not go into 1. Therefore, 0 is written above the division bracket, and the 1 is carried over to the next digit (9) to create 19.

$\begin{array}{r} 2\ 0 \\ 4\overline{)8\ 1\ {}^19\ 2} \end{array}$

4 Divide 19 by the divisor, 4.

4 goes into 19 four times ($4 \times 4 = 16$) with 3 left over so:

$19 \div 4 = \textbf{4}$ remainder 3

Write 4 above the 9 in the division bracket, and carry the remainder (3) over to the next digit (2) to create 32.

$\begin{array}{r} 2\ 0\ 4 \\ 4\overline{)8\ 1\ {}^19\ {}^32} \end{array}$

5 Divide 32 by the divisor (4). 4 goes into 32 eight times so:

$32 \div 4 = 8$

Write 8 above the 2 in the dividend. The division problem is now complete.

$\begin{array}{r} 2\ 0\ 4\ 8 \\ 4\overline{)8\ 1\ {}^19\ {}^32} \end{array}$

$8192 \div 4 = 2048$

Long Multiplication

Multiplication problems with large numbers cannot always be solved mentally. In such instances, long multiplication can be used.

To solve this multiplication problem, follow the steps outlined below.

232×6

1 Rewrite the multiplication problem so that the smaller number is written under the larger number. Both numbers should be right aligned so that digits with the same place value (hundreds, tens, ones) are aligned vertically.

H	T	O
2	3	2
×		6

2 Multiply each digit in the top number by the bottom number. Always multiply from **right to left**.

$2 \times 6 = \textbf{12}$

Write the 2 underneath the ones column and carry the 1 over to the tens column.

Write the carried number here.

H	T	O
2	3	2
×		6
		2
	1	

3 Multiply the next digit, 3, in the top number by the bottom number, 6, and add any carried numbers.

$3 \times 6 = \textbf{18}; \textbf{18} + \textbf{1}$ **(the carried number)** $= \textbf{19}$

Write the 9 underneath the tens column and carry the 1 over to the hundreds column.

Remember to add me!

H	T	O
2	3	2
×		6
	9	2
1	1	

4 Multiply the next digit, 2, in the top number by the bottom number, 6, and add any carried numbers.

$2 \times 6 = \textbf{12}; \textbf{12} + \textbf{1}$ **(the carried number)** $= \textbf{13}$

As there are no more numbers to multiply the whole number can be written underneath. The multiplication problem is now solved.

$232 \times 6 = \textbf{1392}$

H	T	O
2	3	2
×		6
1 3	9	2
1	1	

daydream
EDUCATI

To solve this multiplication problem, follow the steps outlined below. **471 × 52**

1

Rewrite the multiplication problem so that the smaller number is written under the larger number.

Multiply each digit in the top number by the bottom number. Always multiply from **right to left**.

$1 × 2 = 2$

Write the 2 underneath the ones column.

```
    H  T  O
    4  7  1
 ×     5  2
          2
```

2

Working from **right to left**, multiply the next digits in the top number by the bottom number, 2. Remember to add any carried numbers.

$7 × 2 = 14$
$4 × 2 = 8; 8 + 1$ (the carried number) $= 9$
Therefore, $2 × 471 = 942$

```
    H  T  O
    4  7  1
 ×     5  2
    9  4  2
    1
```

3

Before the top number can be multiplied by the next digit in the bottom number, 5, a zero needs to be added in the ones column. This is because the 5 in the bottom number actually represents 50.

It is **vital** that this step is performed or the answer will be incorrect.

```
    H  T  O
    4  7  1
 ×     5  2
    9  4  2
    1
          0
```

4

Now multiply each digit in the top number by 5. Remember to work **from right to left**.

$1 × 5 = 5$
$7 × 5 = 35$
$4 × 5 = 20; 20 + 3$ (the carried number) $= 23$
Therefore, $50 × 471 = 23,550$

```
       H  T  O
       4  7  1
    ×     5  2
       9  4  2
       1
 2  3  5  5  0
    3
```

5

Finally, use column addition to add the two products together.

$2 + 0 = 2$
$4 + 5 = 9$
$9 + 5 = 14$
$3 + 1$ (the carried number) $= 4$
2

Do **not** include these numbers when adding up!

Therefore, $471 × 52 = 24,492$

```
       H  T  O
       4  7  1
    ×     5  2
       9  4  2
       ①
 + 2  3  5  5  0
    ③
 2  4  4  9  2
    1
```

Simple Fractions

When a whole or group is divided into equal parts, a fraction is created.

$$\frac{1}{2}$$

The top number in a fraction is called the **numerator**.

The bottom number in a fraction is called the **denominator**.

This triangle is split into three equal parts. Each part is one-third.

One-third ($\frac{1}{3}$) is purple.
Two-thirds ($\frac{2}{3}$) are red.

This square is split into four equal parts. Each part is one-quarter.

Three-quarters ($\frac{3}{4}$) are green.
One-quarter ($\frac{1}{4}$) is blue.

This pentagon is split into five equal parts. Each part is one-fifth.

Three-fifths ($\frac{3}{5}$) are pink.
Two-fifths ($\frac{2}{5}$) are orange.

Equivalent Fractions

Equivalent fractions have different numerators and denominators but are equal in value. They are created by multiplying or dividing both numbers in the fraction by the same number.

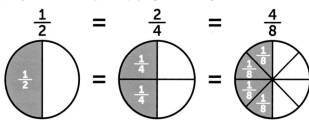

$$\frac{1}{2} = \frac{2}{4} = \frac{4}{8}$$

Look how these fractions take up the same amount of each circle but the numerators and denominators are different.

A fraction wall can be used to help identify equivalent fractions.

$$\frac{1}{2} = \frac{4}{8}$$

$$\frac{1}{3} = \frac{2}{6}$$

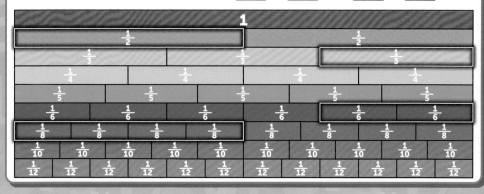

daydream EDUCAT

Simplifying & Ordering Fractions

Simplifying Fractions

To simplify a fraction the **numerator** and **denominator** must be divided by their **highest common factor** (the largest whole number that is a factor of both numbers) to create like fractions.

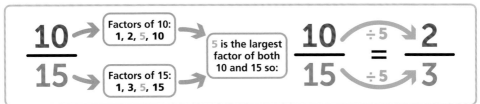

$$\frac{10}{15} \rightarrow$$ Factors of 10: **1, 2, 5, 10**

Factors of 15: **1, 3, 5, 15**

5 is the largest factor of both 10 and 15 so:

$$\frac{10}{15} \quad \overset{\div 5}{\underset{\div 5}{=}} \quad \frac{2}{3}$$

Simplifying in steps

Sometimes it is easier to simplify in steps.

Divide the top and bottom numbers of the fraction by a common factor until they cannot be divided any further.

$$\frac{60}{100} \quad \overset{\div 10}{\underset{\div 10}{=}} \quad \frac{6}{10} \quad \overset{\div 2}{\underset{\div 2}{=}} \quad \frac{3}{5}$$

Ordering Fractions

It is easy to put like fractions (fractions with the same **denominator**) in numerical order.

$$\frac{5}{12} \quad \frac{3}{12} \quad \frac{6}{12} \quad \frac{1}{12} \quad \Rightarrow \quad \frac{1}{12} \quad \frac{3}{12} \quad \frac{5}{12} \quad \frac{6}{12}$$

To order fractions with different denominators, first change all of the fractions so they have the same **denominator**.

1 Identify the lowest common multiple of the **denominators**. The lowest common multiple of **6**, **8** and **4** is **24**.

$$\frac{5}{6} \quad \frac{7}{8} \quad \frac{3}{4}$$

Multiples of 6: **6, 12, 18,** 24
Multiples of 8: **8, 16,** 24, **32**
Multiples of 4: **4, 8, 12, 16, 20,** 24

2 Multiply the fractions by the appropriate numbers so that they share the same denominator, **24**.

$$\frac{5}{6} \overset{\times 4}{\underset{\times 4}{=}} \frac{20}{24} \qquad \frac{7}{8} \overset{\times 3}{\underset{\times 3}{=}} \frac{21}{24} \qquad \frac{3}{4} \overset{\times 6}{\underset{\times 6}{=}} \frac{18}{24}$$

3 Now that the fractions have the same **denominator**, use the **numerators** to place them in order. Then convert them back to their original form.

$$\frac{18}{24} \quad \frac{20}{24} \quad \frac{21}{24}$$

Smallest ⟶ Largest

Convert back to original form.

$$\frac{3}{4} \quad \frac{5}{6} \quad \frac{7}{8}$$

Smallest ⟶ Largest

daydream EDUCATION

Adding & Subtracting Fractions

To add or subtract fractions, their denominators must be the same. Fractions with the same denominator are known as **like fractions**.

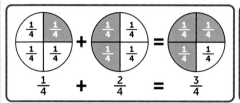

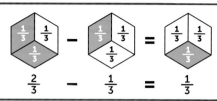

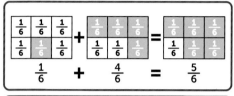

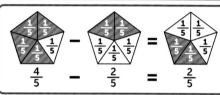

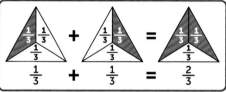

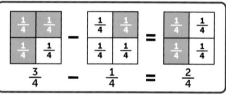

When the denominators are different (unlike fractions), multiply one, or both fractions, so they share the same denominator. To do this, you will need to identify the **lowest common multiple** of each denominator.

$$\frac{1}{4} + \frac{1}{3}$$

Multiples of 4	Multiples of 3
4, 8, 12, 16, 20	3, 6, 9, 12, 15

The lowest common multiple of 3 and 4 is 12. Therefore, multiply the fractions by the appropriate number so that they share the lowest common denominator of 12.

$$\frac{1}{4} \underset{\times 3}{\overset{\times 3}{=}} \frac{3}{12} \qquad \frac{1}{3} \underset{\times 4}{\overset{\times 4}{=}} \frac{4}{12}$$

Add the fractions together to find the answer. Remember to only add the numerators.

$$\frac{3}{12} + \frac{4}{12} = \frac{7}{12}$$

$$\frac{1}{3} - \frac{1}{6}$$

Multiples of 3	Multiples of 6
3, 6, 9	6, 12, 18

The lowest common multiple of 3 and 6 is 6. Therefore, multiply each fraction by the appropriate number so that they share the lowest common denominator of 6.

$$\frac{1}{3} \underset{\times 2}{\overset{\times 2}{=}} \frac{2}{6} \qquad \frac{1}{6} \underset{\times 1}{\overset{\times 1}{=}} \frac{1}{6}$$

Perform the subtraction to find the answer. Remember to only subtract the numerators.

$$\frac{2}{6} - \frac{1}{6} = \frac{1}{6}$$

daydream

Adding Mixed Numbers

To solve this problem, follow the steps outlined below.

$$1\tfrac{3}{4} + 2\tfrac{1}{8}$$

1 Change the mixed numbers into improper fractions.

$$1\tfrac{3}{4} \to \tfrac{4}{4} + \tfrac{3}{4} \to \tfrac{7}{4} \qquad 2\tfrac{1}{8} \to \tfrac{8}{8} + \tfrac{8}{8} + \tfrac{1}{8} \to \tfrac{17}{8}$$

$$\frac{7}{4} + \frac{17}{8}$$

2 If the denominators are different, multiply the fractions so that they share the lowest common denominator.

$$\frac{7}{4} \xrightarrow{\times 2} = \frac{14}{8} \qquad \frac{17}{8}$$

This fraction does not need to change!

3 Add the fractions and then convert the answer back to a mixed number.

8 goes into 31 **3** times with **7** remaining, **therefore:**

$$1\tfrac{3}{4} + 2\tfrac{1}{8} = 3\tfrac{7}{8}$$

$$\frac{14}{8} + \frac{17}{8} = \frac{31}{8}$$

$$\frac{31}{8} = 3\tfrac{7}{8}$$

Subtracting Mixed Numbers

To solve this problem, follow the steps outlined below.

$$2\tfrac{2}{3} - 1\tfrac{1}{2}$$

1 Change the mixed numbers into improper fractions.

$$2\tfrac{2}{3} \to \tfrac{3}{3} + \tfrac{3}{3} + \tfrac{2}{3} \to \tfrac{8}{3} \qquad 1\tfrac{1}{2} \to \tfrac{2}{2} + \tfrac{1}{2} \to \tfrac{3}{2}$$

$$\frac{8}{3} - \frac{3}{2}$$

2 If the denominators are different, multiply the fractions so that they share the lowest common denominator.

$$\frac{8}{3} \xrightarrow{\times 2} = \frac{16}{6} \qquad \frac{3}{2} \xrightarrow{\times 3} = \frac{9}{6}$$

3 Subtract the fraction and then convert the answer back to a mixed number.

6 goes into 7 **once** with **1** remaining, **therefore:**

$$2\tfrac{2}{3} - 1\tfrac{1}{2} = 1\tfrac{1}{6}$$

$$\frac{16}{6} - \frac{9}{6} = \frac{7}{6}$$

$$\frac{7}{6} = 1\tfrac{1}{6}$$

Mixed Numbers & Improper Fractions

Mixed numbers and improper fractions are two different ways of writing fractions that are greater than one, or a whole.

The fraction below can be written as a mixed number or as an improper fraction.

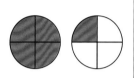

=

Mixed Numbers contain a whole number and a fractional part.

$$1\frac{1}{4}$$

=

Improper Fractions have a numerator that is greater than or equal to the denominator.

$$\frac{5}{4}$$

Converting Improper Fractions to Mixed Numbers

Divide the **numerator** by the **denominator**.

$$\frac{9}{4}$$

4 goes into 9 twice with **1** left over, therefore:

$9 \div 4 = 2$ remainder 1

You now have 2 wholes (ones) and **1** remainder, which becomes the numerator.

$$2\frac{1}{4}$$

The **denominator** does not change.

Therefore:

$$\frac{9}{4} = 2\frac{1}{4}$$

A visual representation of the conversion is shown below.

Converting Mixed Numbers to Improper Fractions

Multiply the **denominator** by the whole number.

$$3\frac{1}{2}$$

$2 \times 3 = 6$

Add this number to the **numerator**.

$6 + 1 = 7$

This creates:

$$\frac{7}{2}$$

Therefore:

$$3\frac{1}{2} = \frac{7}{2}$$

A visual representation of the conversion is shown below.

0    $\frac{1}{2}$ 1 $\frac{1}{2}$ 2 $\frac{1}{2}$ 3 $\frac{1}{2}$ 4 $\frac{1}{2}$

$\frac{0}{2}$ $\frac{1}{2}$ $\frac{2}{2}$ $\frac{3}{2}$ $\frac{4}{2}$ $\frac{5}{2}$ $\frac{6}{2}$ $\frac{7}{2}$ $\frac{8}{2}$ $\frac{9}{2}$

daydream
EDUCATION

Multiplying Fractions

Multiplying Fractions by Whole Numbers

To solve $\frac{2}{5} \times 4$ follow the steps outlined below.

1 Write the whole number as a fraction. 4 becomes the **numerator** and 1 is used as the **denominator**.

$$4 \implies \frac{4}{1}$$

2 Multiply the **numerators** and then the **denominators**.
$2 \times 4 = \mathbf{8}$
$5 \times 1 = \mathbf{5}$

$$\frac{2}{5} \times \frac{4}{1} = \frac{8}{5}$$

3 Convert this answer, $\frac{8}{5}$, into a mixed number by dividing the **numerator** by the **denominator**.

$8 \div 5 = 1$ remainder 3

The remainder, **3**, becomes the **numerator**, and the **denominator**, **5**, does not change.

$\frac{2}{5} \times 4 = \mathbf{1\frac{3}{5}}$

$8 \div 5 = 1$ remainder 3

$$\frac{8}{5} \implies 1\frac{3}{5}$$

Multiplying Mixed Numbers by Whole Numbers

To solve $2\frac{1}{4} \times 3$ follow the steps outlined below.

1 Convert the mixed number into an improper fraction: Multiply the **denominator** by the whole number, and add this to the **numerator**.

$2 \times 4 = 8;\ 8 + 1$ (the numerator) $= \mathbf{9}$

This is used as the **numerator** in the improper fraction.

$$2\frac{1}{4} \implies \frac{9}{4}$$

2 Write the whole number as a fraction. **3** becomes the **numerator** and 1 is the **denominator**.

$$3 \implies \frac{3}{1}$$

3 Multiply the **numerators** and then the **denominators**.
$9 \times 3 = \mathbf{27}$
$4 \times 1 = \mathbf{4}$

$$\frac{9}{4} \times \frac{3}{1} = \frac{27}{4}$$

4 Convert this answer, $\frac{27}{4}$, into a mixed number by dividing the **numerator** by the **denominator**.

$27 \div 4 = 6$ remainder 3

The remainder, **3**, becomes the **numerator**, and the **denominator** does not change.

$2\frac{1}{4} \times 3 = \mathbf{6\frac{3}{4}}$

$27 \div 4 = 6$ remainder 3

$$\frac{27}{4} \implies 6\frac{3}{4}$$

25

Dividing Fractions

Dividing Fractions

$\frac{1}{2} \div \frac{1}{6}$ is asking how many times $\frac{1}{6}$ goes into $\frac{1}{2}$.
This can be easily identified on a fraction wall.

$\frac{1}{6}$ goes into $\frac{1}{2}$ three times

To solve $\frac{4}{7} \div \frac{2}{3}$ follow the steps outlined below.

Step 1
Turn the second fraction upside down, and change the division symbol into a multiplication symbol.

$$\frac{4}{7} \div \frac{2}{3} \Rightarrow \frac{4}{7} \times \frac{3}{2}$$

Step 2
Multiply the numerators together followed by the denominators.

$$\frac{4}{7} \times \frac{3}{2} = \frac{12}{14}$$

Step 3
Simplify if possible.

$$\frac{12}{14} \overset{\div 2}{\underset{\div 2}{=}} \frac{6}{7}$$

Dividing Fractions by Whole Numbers

To divide a fraction by a whole number, multiply the denominator by the whole number and simplify where possible.

$$\frac{1}{2} \div 4 \Rightarrow \frac{1}{2 \times 4} = \frac{1}{8}$$

If you shared $\frac{1}{2}$ a pizza between 4 people, each person would get $\frac{1}{8}$ of the whole pizza.

$\frac{1}{2}$ of a pizza

$\div 4$

$= \frac{1}{8}$ each

daydream EDUCATIO

Fractions Decimals Percentages

Fractions, decimals and percentages are three different ways of expressing a proportion of a whole.

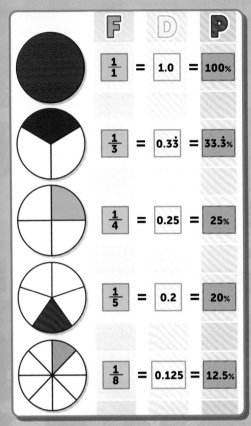

F		D		P
$\frac{1}{1}$	=	1.0	=	100%
$\frac{1}{3}$	=	0.3̇3̇	=	33.3̇%
$\frac{1}{4}$	=	0.25	=	25%
$\frac{1}{5}$	=	0.2	=	20%
$\frac{1}{8}$	=	0.125	=	12.5%

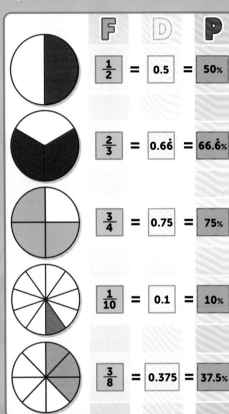

F		D		P
$\frac{1}{2}$	=	0.5	=	50%
$\frac{2}{3}$	=	0.6̇6̇	=	66.6̇%
$\frac{3}{4}$	=	0.75	=	75%
$\frac{1}{10}$	=	0.1	=	10%
$\frac{3}{8}$	=	0.375	=	37.5%

Fraction — Divide numerator by denominator → **Decimal** — Multiply by 100 → **Percentage**

$\frac{1}{5}$ — Convert to a fraction* ← 0.20 — Divide by 100 ← 20%

* To convert a decimal to a fraction:

1 Multiply the decimal by 100 and use it as the numerator.

$0.20 \times 100 = \underline{20}$

2 Use 100 as the denominator.

$\frac{20}{100}$

3 Remember to simplify if possible.

$\frac{20}{100} \begin{array}{c} \rightarrow \div 20 \rightarrow \\ = \\ \rightarrow \div 20 \rightarrow \end{array} \frac{1}{5}$

27

Simple Percentages

The word percent comes from the Latin words *per* and *cent* meaning 'out of every 100'. The symbol for percent is %.

1% **20%** **50%** **100%**

Converting Percentages to Fractions

1 Make the percentage the numerator of the fraction.

$$30\% = \underline{30}$$

2 *Per cent* means 'out of every 100' so 100 is used as the denominator.

$$\frac{30}{100}$$

3 Simplify if possible.

$$\frac{30}{100} \to \div 10 \to = \frac{3}{10} \to \div 10 \to$$

Converting Percentages to Decimals

To convert a percentage to a decimal, remove the percent symbol and divide the percentage by 100.

$$25 \div 100 = 0.25$$
$$25\% = 0.25$$

Finding a Percentage of an Amount

Amelia is buying a new pair of jeans. They cost £40 but have 20% off. What is the sale price?

1 Convert the percentage discount into a decimal.

$$20 \div 100 = 0.2$$

2 Multiply the cost by the decimal number.

$$40 \times 0.2 = 8$$

3 Subtract this amount from the original cost.

$$40 - 8 = £32$$

The sale price of the jeans is **£32**

You can also calculate a percentage by finding 10% first.

1 Find 10% by dividing the price by 10.

$$40 \div 10 = 4$$

2 Multiply by 2 to get 20%.

$$4 \times 2 = 8$$

3 Subtract this amount from the original cost.

$$40 - 8 = £32$$

For more complex calculations, find 1% first. For example, to find 23% of an amount, divide it by 100 (to find 1%) and then multiply by 23.

daydream
EDUCATION

Ratios

A ratio is a way of comparing two or more quantities.

Purple paint is made by mixing blue and red paint at a ratio of 2 to 3.

2:3

To make mortar, sand and cement are mixed at a ratio of 5 to 2.

5:2

Lilly, Jack and Jo have shared the money at a ratio of 2 to 6 to 3.

2:6:3

A ratio must be written in the correct order, with **the quantity mentioned first written first.**

The ratio of cats to dogs is 3:4 ✓

NOT

The ratio of dogs to cats is 3:4 ✗

Note that the ratio of dogs to cats is **4:3**.

Ratios are easier to work out when they are in their simplest form. To simplify ratios, both numbers must be **divided by their highest common factor.**

The ratio of blue to red tiles is 6 to 3 but this can be simplified.

3 is the highest common factor of 6 and 3, so divide both numbers by 3.

6:3
÷3   ÷3
2:1

Can you simplify these ratios to their simplest form?

6:4   **9:3**   **2:8:4**

daydream EDUCATION

Scale

Scale and ratio have similar principles.
If the ratio of A to B is 1:2, A is half the size of B, or B is twice the size of A.

The plan of Oliver's bedroom is drawn at a scale of **1:50**.
This means that the bedroom is 50 times bigger in real life than in the drawing.

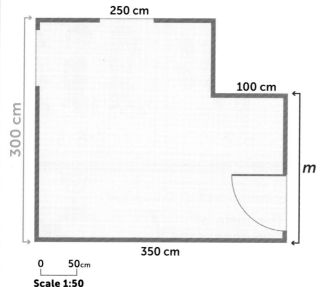

250 cm

100 cm

300 cm

m

350 cm

0   50 cm

Scale 1:50

To identify the length of **300 cm** on the drawing, divide the real-life measurement by the scale:

$300 \text{ cm} \div 50 = \textbf{6 cm}$

To identify the length of *m* in real-life, use a ruler to measure the length of *m* on the drawing (in this case **4 cm**) and multiply it by the scale:

$4 \text{ cm} \times 50 = \textbf{200 cm}$

Using Scales to Draw and Read Maps

The map below has a scale of **1:50,000**.
This means the map is 50,000 times smaller than the actual area shown.

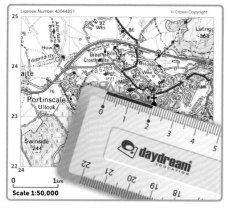

0   1 km

Scale 1:50,000

On the map the campsite is 2 cm from the church. To calculate the actual distance, multiply the measurement by the scale:

2 cm × Scale
$2 \text{ cm} \times 50,000 = \textbf{100,000 cm}$

Convert the measurement to the correct unit:

$100,000 \text{ cm} = \textbf{1 km}$

Therefore, the campsite is 1 km from the church.

daydream
EDUCATIO

Algebra

The word algebra comes from the Arabic term *al-jabr* which means 'the reunion of broken parts'.

In algebra, letters are used to represent unknown numbers, or variables.

 1 **Think of a number. Let's call it 'y'.** y

2 **Double it (multiply by 2).** $2 \times y$

3 Add 4. $2y + 4$

So $2y + 4 = 10$
This is called an equation.

Solving an equation means finding the value of the variable, y.
To find the value of y, perform the steps above in reverse.
You basically undo the equation.

3 Subtract 4.
$$2y + 4$$
$$- 4$$
$$= 2y$$

2 **Halve it (divide by 2).**
$$2y$$
$$\div 2$$
$$= y$$

1 y **represents the number 3.** y

Solving Equations

Inverse operations are opposite operations that 'undo' each other.

Addition and Subtraction are inverse operations.

12

$+4$ $8 + 4 = 12$ -4
         $12 - 4 = 8$

8

Multiplication and Division are inverse operations.

15

$\times 5$ $3 \times 5 = 15$ $\div 5$
              $15 \div 5 = 3$

3

How to Solve Equations With Inverse Operations

The aim when solving an equation is to get the **variable** by itself on one side of the equation with a **number** on the other side – for example, $x = 2$.

When there are other operations on the same side of an equation as the variable, they need to be removed. This is done by performing the opposite of the operation acting upon the variable. **This must be done to both sides of the equation.**

$n + 3 = 12$	$x - 7 = 1$	$5 \times y = 20$	$m \div 5 = 3$
The inverse of addition is subtraction, so **subtract 3 from both sides of the equation.**	The inverse of subtraction is addition, so **add 7 to both sides of the equation.**	The inverse of multiplication is division, so divide both sides of the equation by 5.	The inverse of division is multiplication, so **multiply both sides of the equation by 5.**
$n + 3 = 12$	$x - 7 = 1$	$5 \times y = 20$	$m \div 5 = 3$
-3 -3	$+7$ $+7$	$\div 5$ $\div 5$	$\times 5$ $\times 5$
$n = 9$	$x = 8$	$y = 4$	$m = 15$

The above rules do not always work for division and subtraction.
When the **variable** is the divisor, or being subtracted, solve the problem in two steps.

When the variable is being subtracted:	**When the variable is the divisor:**
Add d to both sides of the equation.	Multiply both sides of the equation by w.
$7 - d = 4$	$12 \div w = 3$
$+d$ $+d$	$\times w$ $\times w$
$7 = 4 + d$	$12 = 3w$
Subtract 4 from both sides of the equation.	Divide both sides of the equation by 3.
-4 -4	$\div 3$ $\div 3$
$3 = d$	$4 = w$

daydream EDUCATIO

Max and Amy have 37 apps in total.
If Amy has 21 apps, how many does Max have?

1. Turn the question into an equation.

Use m to represent the unknown value (the number of apps Max has).	Max has __ apps	Amy has 21 apps	37 apps in total
	m +	21 =	37

2. Solve the equation to find the value of m.

Subtraction is the inverse operation of addition so **subtract 21 from both sides of the equation.**	$m \quad + \quad 21 \quad = \quad 37$
	$ \quad -21 \qquad -21$
	$m \qquad\qquad\qquad = \quad 16$

The equation is now solved. m = 16 so Max has 16 apps.

Rohan has three pieces of wood of equal length, and one 6 cm piece.
The total length of the four pieces of wood is 42 cm.

How long is each of the three equal pieces of wood?

1. Turn the question into an equation.

Use w to represent the unknown value (the length of the three equal pieces of wood).	3 pieces of wood	Other piece of wood	Total length
	$3 \times w$ +	6 =	42

2. Solve the equation to find the value of w.

Subtraction is the inverse operation of addition so **subtract 6 from both sides of the equation.**	$3w \quad + \quad 6 \quad = \quad 42$
	$ \quad -6 \qquad\quad -6$
	$3w \qquad\qquad = \quad 36$
Division is the inverse operation of multiplication so **divide both sides of the equation by 3.**	$\div 3 \qquad\qquad \div 3$
	$w \qquad\qquad = \quad 12$

The equation is now solved. w = 12 so each equal piece of wood is 12 cm long.

daydream EDUCATION

Number Sequences

A number sequence in which each number increases (or decreases) by the same amount each time is called a **linear sequence**. The amount the sequence increases (or decreases) by is known as the **common difference**.

Common Difference

To find the common difference, you need to find the difference between each term (number) in the sequence.

Finding the common difference enables you to work out the missing numbers in a sequence. To find the next term in a sequence, add (or subtract) the common difference.

The next term in this sequence is 20 because 16 + 4 = **20**

32 30 28 26 ?

 − 2   − 2   − 2   − 2

The next term in this sequence is 24 because 26 − 2 = **24**

The same rule can be used to find a missing number in the middle of a sequence.

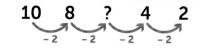

The missing term in this sequence is 20 because 15 + 5 = **20**

10 8 ? 4 2

 − 2   − 2   − 2   − 2

The missing term in this sequence is 6 because 8 − 2 = **6**

Square Numbers

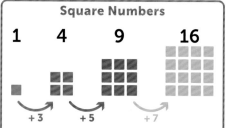

The difference between each number in the sequence is an odd number that increases by **2**.

Triangle Numbers

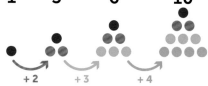

The difference between each number in the sequence increases by **1**.

daydream EDUCATION

Measurement

Length

The metric units of length are:
millimetre (mm), **centimetre (cm)**, **metre (m)** and **kilometre (km)**.

10 mm = **1 cm**	**100 cm** = 1 m	1,000 m = 1 km

Although you divide to convert to a larger unit, this does not mean that 1 mm is longer than 1 cm. 1 mm is ten times shorter than 1 cm.

$\div 10$ $\div 100$ $\div 1000$

mm cm m km

$\times 10$ $\times 100$ $\times 1000$

Although you multiply to convert to a smaller unit, this does not mean that 1 km is shorter than 1 m. 1 km is 1,000 times longer than 1 m.

Ellis jumped:
2,250 mm = 225 cm = 2.25 m

Jessica ran:
12,000 m = 12 km

Mass

The metric units of mass are:
grams (g) and **kilograms (kg)**.

1,000 g = 1 kg

$\div 1000$

g kg

$\times 1000$

750 g = 0.75 kg   **5,000 g = 5 kg**   **80,000 g = 80 kg**

Capacity

The metric units of capacity are:
millilitres (ml) and **litres (l)**.

1,000 ml = 1 l

$\div 1000$

ml l

$\times 1000$

   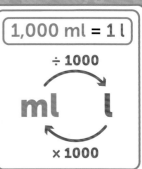

100 ml = 0.1 l   **330 ml = 0.33 l**   **20,000 ml = 20 l**

35

Measurement Conversion

Length

2.54 centimetres (cm)	≈	1 inch (in)

÷ 2.54

12.7 cm ≈ 5 in

× 2.54

The pen is 12.7 centimetres, or 5 inches, long.

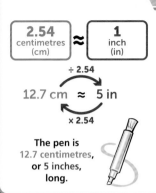

1 metre (m)	≈	1.1 yards (yd)

× 1.1

100 m ≈ 110 yd

÷ 1.1

The pitch is 100 metres, or 110 yards, long.

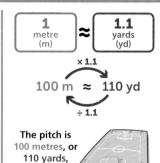

1.6 kilometres (km)	≈	1 mile (mi)

÷ 1.6

184 km ≈ 115 mi

× 1.6

It is 184 kilometres, or 115 miles, from Bath to London.

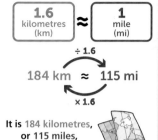

Mass

28.35 grams (g)	≈	1 ounce (oz)

÷ 28.35

340.2 g ≈ 12 oz

× 28.35

The jar holds 340.2 grams, or 12 ounces, of jam.

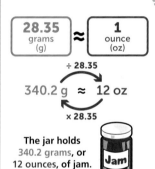

1 kilogram (kg)	≈	2.2 pounds (lb)

× 2.2

5 kg ≈ 11 lb

÷ 2.2

The cat weighs 5 kilograms, or 11 pounds.

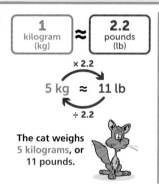

6.4 kilograms (kg)	≈	1 stone (st)

÷ 6.4

57.6 kg ≈ 9 st

× 6.4

Sally weighs 57.6 kilograms, or 9 stone.

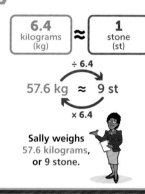

Capacity/Volume

568 millilitres (ml)	≈	1 pint (pt)

÷ 568

1,136 ml ≈ 2 pt

× 568

The jug has a capacity of 1,136 millilitres, or 2 pints.

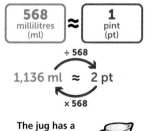

1 litre (l)	≈	1.76 pints (pt)

× 1.76

2 l ≈ 3.52 pt

÷ 1.76

The kettle has a capacity of 2 litres, or 3.52 pints.

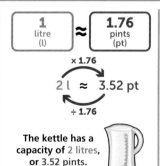

4.5 litres (l)	≈	1 gallon (gal)

÷ 4.5

180 l ≈ 40 gal

× 4.5

The bath has a capacity of 180 litres, or 40 gallons.

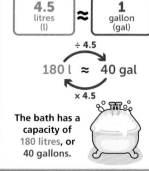

Metric   Imperial

daydream
EDUCATI

Time

| 60 seconds = 1 minute | 60 minutes = 1 hour | 24 hours = 1 day |

Analogue Clocks

The short hand is the hour hand. It takes 1 hour to move from one number to the next.

The long hand is the minute hand. It takes 60 minutes to go all the way around the clock.

The 12 longer or bolder lines on a clock each represent 1 hour intervals for the small hand, or 5 minute intervals for the minute hand.

The 60 small lines on a clock each represent one minute. It takes the minute hand 60 seconds to move between each pair of lines.

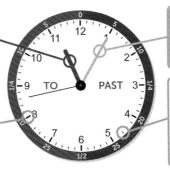

7:10
Ten minutes past seven.

3:20
Twenty minutes past three.

10:50
Ten minutes to eleven.

Digital Clocks

Digital clocks display the time digitally as numbers.

On a 12-hour digital clock, 12 hours are a.m. and 12 hours are p.m.

On a 24-hour digital clock, there are 24 hours and no a.m. or p.m.

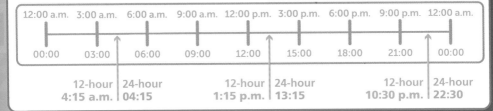

12:00 a.m.	3:00 a.m.	6:00 a.m.	9:00 a.m.	12:00 p.m.	3:00 p.m.	6:00 p.m.	9:00 p.m.	12:00 a.m.
00:00	03:00	06:00	09:00	12:00	15:00	18:00	21:00	00:00

12-hour	24-hour	12-hour	24-hour	12-hour	24-hour
4:15 a.m.	04:15	1:15 p.m.	13:15	10:30 p.m.	22:30

Money

| 1p | 2p | 5p | 10p | 20p | 50p | £1 | £2 |

£5   £10   £20

You can use a wide variety of coins to make a set amount of money.

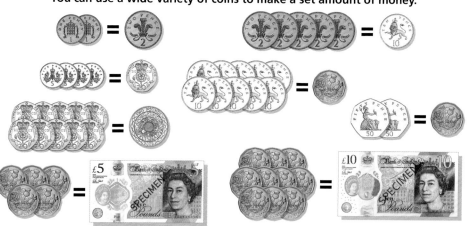

Try to make £12.45 using the fewest number of coins and notes!

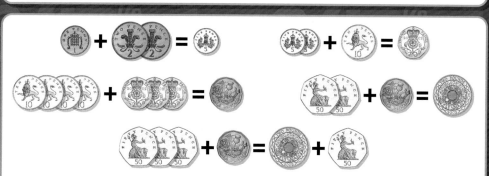

How many different ways can you make £1 using the coins above?

Photocopying or scanning this image is a breach of copyright law.

daydream
EDUCATION

Perimeter and Area

Perimeter

Perimeter is the total distance around a shape's outer edge.
To calculate the perimeter of a shape, add together the lengths of all the sides.

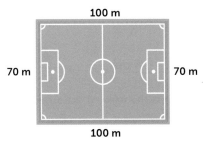

The perimeter of the football field is 340 m:
$$100 + 100 + 70 + 70 = 340 \text{ m}$$

The perimeter of the kite is 190 cm:
$$30 + 30 + 65 + 65 = 190 \text{ cm}$$

Area

Area is the total size of a surface. It is the amount of space inside the perimeter.

12 cm

Width (w)

5 cm

Length (l)

The area of a **rectangle** can be calculated by using the following formula:

$$\text{Area} = \text{length} \times \text{width}$$
$$= l \times w$$
$$= 12 \times 5$$
$$= 60 \text{ cm}^2$$

The area of the rectangle is 60 cm².

When measuring the area of a compound shape, break it down into simpler shapes and then add the areas together. Look at the plan of the room below.

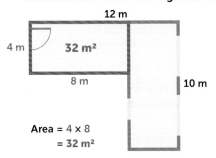

Area = 4 × 8
= 32 m²

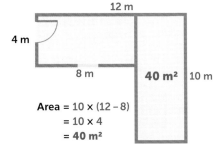

Area = 10 × (12 − 8)
= 10 × 4
= 40 m²

Total area of the compound shape: 32 m² + 40 m² = 72 m²

daydream
EDUCATION

Area and Volume

Rectangle/Square

Area of rectangle = length × width

70 m

100 m

What is the area of the football field?

Area of rectangle = $l \times w$

= 100×70

Area of field = **7,000 m²**

Triangle

Area of triangle = $\frac{1}{2}$ × base × height

24 cm

32 cm

What is the area of the sign?

Area of triangle = $\frac{1}{2} \times b \times h$

= $\frac{1}{2} \times 32 \times 24$

Area of sign = **384 cm²**

Parallelogram

Area of parallelogram = base × height

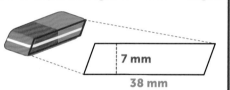

7 mm

38 mm

What is the area of the side face of the rubber?

Area of parallelogram = $b \times h$

= 38×7

Area of rubber = **266 mm²**

Trapezium

Area of trapezium = $\frac{1}{2}$ × (a + b) × height

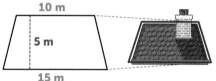

10 m

5 m

15 m

What is the area of the roof?

Area of trapezium = $\frac{1}{2} \times (a + b) \times h$

= $\frac{1}{2} \times (10 + 15) \times 5$

= $\frac{1}{2} \times (25) \times 5$

Area of roof = **62.5 m²**

Volumes of Cubes and Cuboids

Volume of cuboid = length × width × height

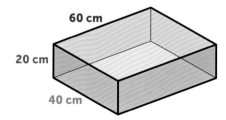

60 cm

20 cm

40 cm

What is the volume of this box?

Volume of cuboid = $l \times w \times h$

= $60 \times 40 \times 20$

Volume of box = **48,000 cm³**

daydream
EDUCATION

Get in Shape

Square

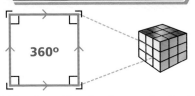

360°

- 4 sides of equal length
- 4 equal angles of 90°
- 4 corners (vertices)
- 2 pairs of parallel sides

Rectangle

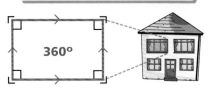

360°

- Opposite sides of equal length
- 4 equal angles of 90°
- 4 corners (vertices)
- 2 pairs of parallel sides

Equilateral Triangle

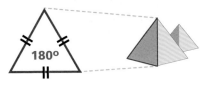

180°

- 3 sides of equal length
- 3 equal angles of 60°
- 3 corners (vertices)
- No parallel sides

Circle

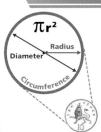

πr^2

Radius
Diameter
Circumference

- **Circumference** – the outer edge of a circle
- **Diameter** – the distance from one edge of a circle to another, passing through the centre
- **Radius** – the distance from the centre of a circle to its edge

Regular Pentagon

540°

- 5 sides of equal length
- 5 equal angles of 108°
- 5 corners (vertices)
- No parallel sides

Regular Hexagon

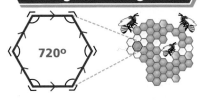

720°

- 6 sides of equal length
- 6 equal angles of 120°
- 6 corners (vertices)
- 3 pairs of parallel sides

Regular Octagon

1080°

- 8 sides of equal length
- 8 equal angles of 135°
- 8 corners (vertices)
- 4 pairs of parallel sides

Trapezium

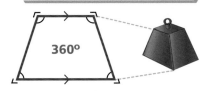

360°

- 4 sides of varying length (2 may be equal)
- 2 pairs of equal angles
- 4 corners (vertices)
- 1 pair of parallel sides

Quadrilaterals

Quadrilaterals have 4 sides and 4 angles. The angles always add up to 360°.

Square

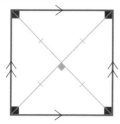

4 equal sides
4 right angles (90°)
Opposite sides are parallel
Diagonals are equal and bisect each other at 90°

Rectangle

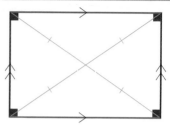

Opposite sides are equal
4 right angles (90°)
Opposite sides are parallel
Diagonals are equal and bisect each other

Rhombus

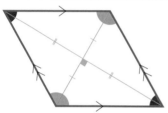

4 equal sides
Opposite angles are equal
Opposite sides are parallel
Diagonals are not equal (unless the rhombus is a square) but bisect each other at 90°

Parallelogram

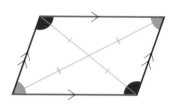

Opposite sides are equal
Opposite angles are equal
Opposite sides are parallel
Diagonals are not equal (unless the parallelogram is a rectangle) but bisect each other

Trapezium

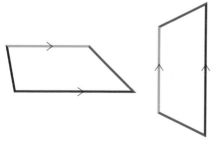

4 sides of varying lengths
One pair of opposite sides are parallel

Kite

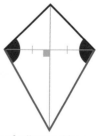

2 pairs of adjacent sides are equal
1 diagonal bisects the other at 90°
1 pair of opposite angles is equal

daydrean
EDUCATIO

Types of Triangles

Equilateral

(*Equi* = Equal, *Lateral* = Sides)

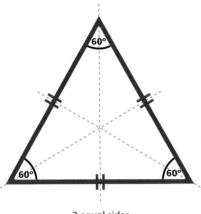

3 equal sides.
3 equal interior angles (each 60°).
3 lines of symmetry.

Isosceles

(Greek for 'two equal sides')

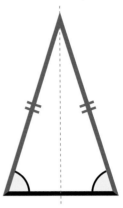

2 equal sides.
2 equal interior angles (base angles).
1 line of symmetry.

Right Angle

(Right angle = 90°)

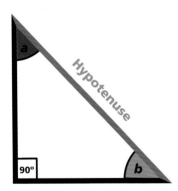

One interior angle is a right angle (90°).
The two other angles add up to 90° ($a + b = 90°$).
There is no symmetry unless angles a and b are 45°.
The longest side is called the hypotenuse.

Scalene

(*Skalēnos*, unequal in Greek)

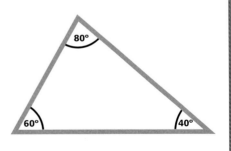

All interior angles are different.
All sides are different.
There are no lines of symmetry.

Remember: The interior angles of a triangle add up to 180°.

Solids and their Nets

A solid figure has flat surfaces (faces), edges and corners (vertices).
A net is the surface of a solid shape folded out flat.

Cube

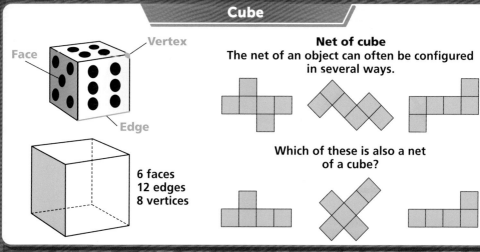

Face
Vertex
Edge

6 faces
12 edges
8 vertices

Net of cube
The net of an object can often be configured in several ways.

Which of these is also a net of a cube?

Triangular Prism

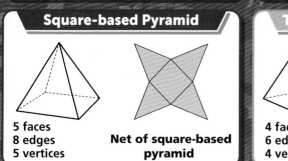

5 faces
9 edges
6 vertices

Net of prism

Cuboid

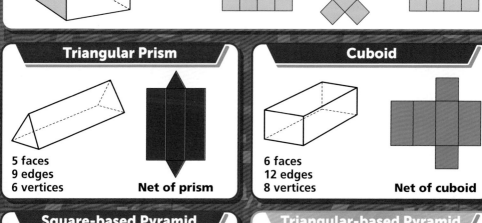

6 faces
12 edges
8 vertices

Net of cuboid

Square-based Pyramid

5 faces
8 edges
5 vertices

Net of square-based pyramid

Triangular-based Pyramid

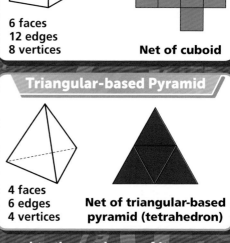

4 faces
6 edges
4 vertices

Net of triangular-based pyramid (tetrahedron)

The surface area of a solid figure is equal to the total area of its net.
Work out the areas of the separate parts of the net and add them all together.

daydrean
EDUCATIO

Polygons

Polygons are 2D shapes that have three sides or more,
are made of straight lines and are closed (with no open sides).

Regular Polygons

A polygon is regular if all of its sides and interior angles are equal.

Triangle

3 sides, 3 equal angles

Quadrilateral

4 sides, 4 equal angles

Pentagon

5 sides, 5 equal angles

Hexagon

6 sides, 6 equal angles

Heptagon

7 sides, 7 equal angles

Octagon

8 sides, 8 equal angles

Irregular Polygons

An irregular polygon can have sides of any length and interior angles of any size.

Triangle **Quadrilateral** **Pentagon** **Hexagon** **Heptagon** **Octagon**

Not Polygons

Curved Shapes **3D Shapes** **Open Shapes**

Symmetry

Line Symmetry

A line of symmetry, also known as a line of reflection, divides an object into two parts that are the same size and shape.

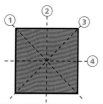

A square has 4 lines of symmetry.

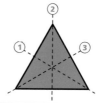

An equilateral triangle has 3 lines of symmetry.

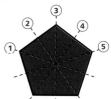

A regular pentagon has 5 lines of symmetry.

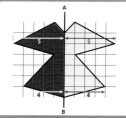

This shape has one line of symmetry. All corresponding parts are equidistant from the line of symmetry.

The butterfly offers an example of line symmetry that occurs in nature. It has one line of symmetry.

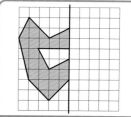

Can you complete this shape? Remember, all corresponding parts should be equidistant from the line of symmetry.

Rotational Symmetry

An object has rotational symmetry if it returns to its original form at any point when it is rotated around a central point. Shapes that have no rotational symmetry have rotational symmetry of order 1.

The square has rotational symmetry of order 4.

It returns to its original form after every 90° rotation.

The letter H has rotational symmetry of order 2.

It returns to its original form after every 180° rotation.

The recycling symbol has rotational symmetry of order 3.

It returns to its original form after every 120° rotation.

The flower has rotational symmetry of order 6.

It returns to its original form after every 60° rotation.

The order of rotational symmetry of any regular polygon is the same as the number of lines of symmetry it has and the number of sides.

daydream
EDUCATI

Angle Properties

Take a triangle

Angles in a triangle add up to 180°

Tear off the angles

They add up to 180°

Angles on a straight line add up to 180°

Take a quadrilateral
Angles in a quadrilateral add up to 360°

Tear off the angles
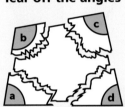

They add up to 360°
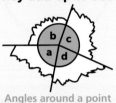
Angles around a point add up to 360°

Angle Properties of Parallel Lines

Corresponding Angles
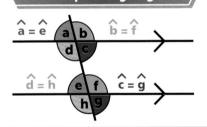
$\hat{a} = \hat{e}$ $\hat{b} = \hat{f}$
$\hat{d} = \hat{h}$ $\hat{c} = \hat{g}$

Vertically Opposite Angles
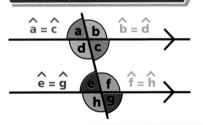
$\hat{a} = \hat{c}$ $\hat{b} = \hat{d}$
$\hat{e} = \hat{g}$ $\hat{f} = \hat{h}$

Alternate Angles
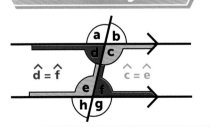
$\hat{d} = \hat{f}$ $\hat{c} = \hat{e}$

Interior Angles
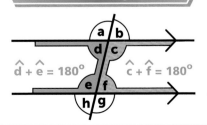
$\hat{d} + \hat{e} = 180°$ $\hat{c} + \hat{f} = 180°$

daydream EDUCATION

Angles and Their Measurement

The turn, or rotation, between two meeting lines is called an angle.
Angles are measured in degrees (°), often with a protractor or angle measurer.

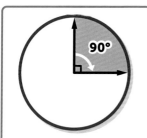

There are **90°** in one-quarter of a rotation.

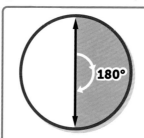

There are **180°** in half a rotation.

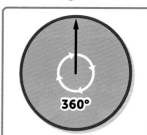

There are **360°** in one complete rotation.

Acute Angles

Angles less than 90° are called **acute angles**.

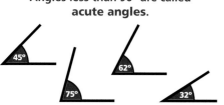

Right Angles

Angles that are 90° are **right angles** and are marked with a small square.

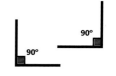

Obtuse Angles

Angles greater than 90° but less than 180° are called obtuse angles.

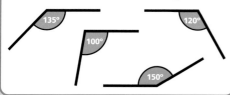

Reflex Angles

Angles greater than 180° are called reflex angles.

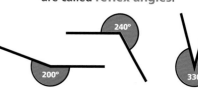

Can you estimate and measure the size of these angles here?
Are they **acute**, obtuse, **reflex** or **right angles**?

daydream
EDUCATION

Graphs and Coordinates

Coordinates are used to represent the position of a point or object on a graph. A graph is made up of an x-axis and a y-axis.

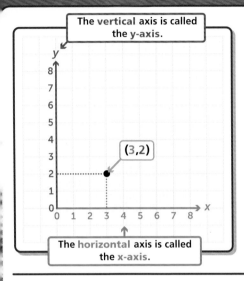

The vertical axis is called the y-axis.

(3,2)

The horizontal axis is called the x-axis.

The first number is the x-coordinate. It gives the horizontal position of the point.

(x,y)

The second number is the y-coordinate. It gives the vertical position of the point.

It is vital that the coordinates are written in the correct order. Think of the alphabet:

x before y

The coordinates of the point on the graph are (3,2).

3 → then 2 ↑

The x-axis and y-axis can be extended to create four quadrants.

Quadrant 2
x is negative
y is positive.

The coordinates of the ship are (-2,3)

Quadrant 3
x is negative
y is negative.

The coordinates of the treasure are (-2,-4)

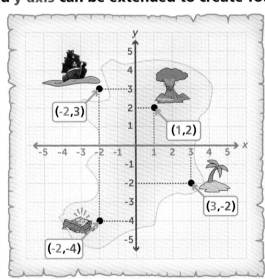

(-2,3)

(1,2)

(3,-2)

(-2,-4)

Quadrant 1
x is positive
y is positive.

The coordinates of the volcano are (1,2)

Quadrant 4
x is positive
y is negative.

The coordinates of the tree are (3,-2)

To help you remember the order in which coordinates are written, remember the saying "along the corridor and up the stairs".

Transformations

A translation moves every point on a shape the same distance in the same direction.

Shape **A** has been translated +3 units along the x-axis and +2 units up the y-axis.

Shape **C** has been translated -6 units along the x-axis and +3 units up the y-axis.

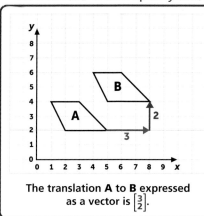

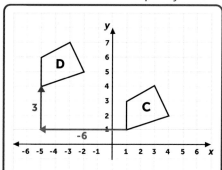

The translation **A** to **B** expressed as a vector is $\begin{bmatrix} 3 \\ 2 \end{bmatrix}$.

The translation **C** to **D** expressed as a vector is $\begin{bmatrix} -6 \\ 3 \end{bmatrix}$.

In a translation, the size, shape and orientation of the shapes are the same. You can turn, flip or move one shape so it fits exactly on the other. Therefore, they are congruent.

Reflection

A reflection produces a mirror image of a shape along a line of reflection.

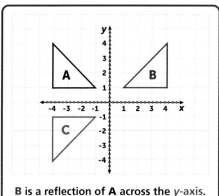

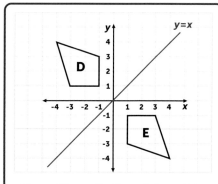

B is a reflection of **A** across the y-axis.
C is a reflection of **A** across the x-axis.

Shape **E** is a reflection of shape **D** in the line y=x.

In a reflection, the positions and orientations of the shapes are different but their size and shape are the same. You can turn, flip or move one shape so it fits exactly on the other. Therefore, they are congruent.

daydream
EDUCATI

Averages

An average is a measure of the central value of a set of data.

Mean

The **mean** of a data set is the **sum of values** divided by the **number of values**.

$$\text{Mean} = \frac{\text{Sum of values}}{\text{Number of values}}$$

The test results for eight pupils are shown below.

Count the number of values to ensure that none are missing!

Calculate the mean by dividing the sum of values by the number of values.

$$\text{Mean} = \frac{49 + 56 + 63 + 67 + 71 + 80 + 82 + 92}{8} = \frac{560}{8} = 70$$

The mean test result is 70

The points scored by a basketball team in their last six games are shown below.

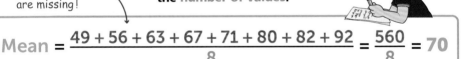

Calculate the mean by dividing the sum of values by the number of values.

Count the number of values to ensure that none are missing!

$$\text{Mean} = \frac{78 + 86 + 96 + 98 + 102 + 110}{6} = \frac{570}{6} = 95$$

The mean number of points scored per game is 95

daydream
EDUCATION

51

Displaying Data

Data is a series of observations, facts or statistics. Raw data can be difficult to understand and read. As a result, it is often organised in graphs and tables.

Frequency Tables

A **frequency table** is used to record how often a value (or set of values) occurs. Frequency tables can be arranged in rows or columns. The frequency tables below show the number of computers owned by a group of students.

No. of computers	Frequency
0	0
1	5
2	8
3	7
4	2

No. of computers	0	1	2	3	4
Frequency	0	5	8	7	2

Sometimes, it is easier to count the frequency with a tally, as follows:

No. of computers	0	1	2	3	4
Tally		JHT	JHT III	JHT II	II
Frequency	0	5	8	7	2

Based on the tables above, how many students own 2 computers?

Data from tables can be displayed in a variety of graphs and charts.

Pictograms

Pictograms use pictures to represent data.

Pupil's Favourite Ice Cream Flavours

Flavour		Frequency
Chocolate	🍦🍦🍦🍦	16
Vanilla	🍦🍦🍦	10
Strawberry	🍦🍦🍦	12
Mint	🍦🍦	6
Raspberry	🍦	2
Bubble Gum	🍦🍦	8

🍦 = 4 pupils

Bar Charts

Bar charts can be used to display grouped data.

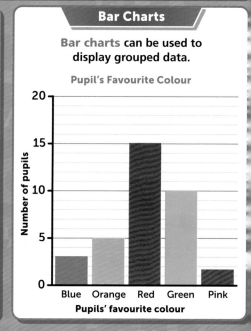

Pupil's Favourite Colour

daydream EDUCATION

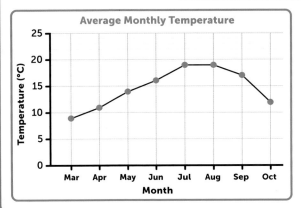

Average Monthly Temperature

In a **line graph**, data is plotted as a series of points that are joined with straight lines.

Line graphs are often used to show change over time.

This graph shows the average monthly temperature in London over eight months.

What was the average monthly temperature in June?

Pie Charts

A **pie chart** is a circular chart that is split into sections to show proportion. The table below shows pupils' favourite sport. Follow the steps to create a pie chart for this data.

Step 1. Divide **each frequency** by the **total number of people surveyed, 30.**

Step 2. In a pie chart, data needs to be represented as a proportion of 360, as there are 360° in a circle.

Therefore, you need to multiply the decimal proportions for each sport by 360.

$0.133 \times 360 = 48$

Sport	Frequency	Frequency ÷ Total	Proportion of 360
Rugby	4	4 ÷ 30 = **0.133**	48
Football	8	8 ÷ 30 = **0.267**	96
Cricket	4	4 ÷ 30 = **0.133**	48
Netball	6	6 ÷ 30 = **0.20**	72
Swimming	3	3 ÷ 30 = **0.10**	36
Tennis	2	2 ÷ 30 = **0.067**	24
Hockey	3	3 ÷ 30 = **0.10**	36
Total	30	30 ÷ 30 = **1**	360

Step 3. Now that the sports have been converted to proportions of 360, the pie chart can be drawn.

Start by drawing a straight line from the centre of the circle to the edge.

Use a protractor to measure and mark the angles for each sport, and label them accordingly.

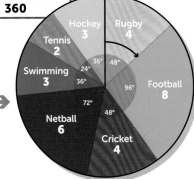

Notes